Learning in Early Years

Enhancing Provision Through
Minibeasts
Ideas to Target Learning and Challenge Thinking

Nicky Simmons & Ginny Morris

Morris & Simmons Education

First Edition: September 2016

@2016 Nicky Simmons & Ginny Morris
All rights reserved

ISBN: 1537458418
ISBN-13: 978-1537458410

About The Authors

Ginny Morris

Ginny has a wide range of experience teaching Early Years in both mainstream and special school settings.

She was the leader of a highly successful Foundation Unit for seven years, during which time she also supported and mentored other Early Years settings within the Local Authority.

Nicky Simmons

Nicky was a Primary School Head Teacher for ten years. During her headship she provided a strategic vision for the school, transforming it into a dynamic learning environment.

She was known for her charismatic style and solution focused approach.

We now run our own company, Morris & Simmons Education. We write & deliver a wide program of professional development workshops & produce our own creative resources for Early Years practitioners.

As well as creating and delivering our own training programmes, we are also regularly invited to work in different settings on Improvement Projects. We offer simple solutions, model good practice and coach practitioners to help them improve their provision.

We are delighted to be able to share our knowledge, experience and expertise with a wider audience through our publications. For more information about our work visit our website www.morrissimmons.com or email mse@morrissimmons.com

Acknowledgements

Throughout our careers we have been privileged to work with so many talented colleagues, children and families, many of whom have significantly contributed to our expertise. We are very grateful for their challenge, inspiration and belief in our abilities, always pushing us to reach new heights.

A special thank you goes to Hockley Heath Primary Academy and Kilsby Primary School. We really appreciate the time these settings took to set up and deliver our ideas providing invaluable feedback and some great photographs. We couldn't have done it without you!

We would also like to thank Stoke Primary School and Holbrook Primary School who took the time to provide us with very valuable feedback on this publication.

Finally we would like to thank our families without whose support, encouragement and technical expertise none of this work would have been possible.

How To Use This Book

Our 'Learning in Early Years' series was written following our highly successful publication '**Planning for Learning in Early Years**'.

We had lots of requests asking for practical advice about how and what to provide in continuous provision in order to help children meet their next steps in learning and make accelerated progress. We observed that learning led by the adult was often well planned for and learning was explicit. However, the learning in continuous provision was often diluted and activities were simply 'nice to have'.

Our work supporting practitioners with planning their provision inspired us to write books that:

- Target learning by exemplifying "**I am learning to…**" statements
- Provide open-ended ideas
- Challenge children to think more deeply

Each book in the series provides a selection of open-ended challenges that can be flexibly used as part of continuous provision. The are designed to be delivered both indoors and outside. They will give busy practitioners an excellent starting point for planning their provision.

The challenges are laid out in an easy to use grid which helps practitioners to know:

- How to resource and set up the challenge
- The specific learning each challenge could possibly target
- How maths and writing skills can be applied across areas of learning

We would strongly advise that you choose one area from the suggested focused learning possibilities section that is most appropriate for your children's next steps, so observations are focused and learning does not become diluted.

Each book in the series is easy to use and intended to inspire both adults and children. Pick and choose the ideas so that they match your children's interests and challenge them to achieve their next steps in learning.

Contents

Areas of Learning: An Overview 1

I Spy Minibeasts 3

Malleable Minibeasts 5

Create a 3D Web 7

Digging for Worms 9

Wash the Spider Down the Spout 11

Sensory Painting 13

Snail Slime 15

Spider Games 17

Symmetrical Minibeasts 19

Spiral Patterns 21

Spider Adventures 23

Feed the Worms 25

Thread a Minibeast 27

Magnetic Minibeasts 29

Create a 2D Web 31

Worm Trails 33

Minibeast Maths 35

Name the Minibeast 37

Catch the Minibeast 39

Areas of Learning: An Overview

Area of Learning		Challenges
PSED	Making Relationships	Spider Games, Minibeast Maths, Catch the Minibeast
	Self-Confidence & Self-Awareness	Feed the Worms
	Managing Feelings & Behaviour	Spider Adventures
Communication & Language	Listening & Attention	I Spy Minibeasts
	Speaking	Malleable Minibeasts, Digging for Worms, Wash the Spider Down the Spout, Sensory Painting, Spider Adventures, Magnetic Minibeasts
	Understanding	
Physical Development	Moving & Handling	Malleable Minibeasts, Create a 3D Web, Digging for Worms, Wash the Spider Down the Spout, Snail Slime, Symmetrical Minibeasts, Thread a Minibeast, Create a 2D Web, Worm Trails, Name the Minibeast, Catch the Minibeast
	Health & Self-Care	
Literacy	Reading	I Spy Minibeasts, Name the Minibeast
	Writing	I Spy Minibeasts
Mathematics	Number	Spider Games, Thread a Minibeast, Magnetic Minibeasts, Minibeast Maths
	Shape, Space & Measure	Wash the Spider Down the Spout, Snail Slime, Symmetrical Minibeasts, Spiral Patterns, Catch the Minibeast
Understanding the World	People & Communities	
	The World	Malleable Minibeasts, Digging for Worms, Sensory Painting, Create a 2D Web
	Technology	
Expressive Arts & Design	Using Media & Materials	Sensory Painting, Snail Slime, Symmetrical Minibeasts, Spiral Patterns, Worm Trails
	Being Imaginative	Create a 3D Web, Feed the Worms

1KG ℮

Cherry & Cola Bottle Mix
Product of the EU

Challenge: **I Spy Minibeasts**　　　　Suggested Area of Provision: **Small World**

Enhance with:	Invite your children to:	Other enhancements:
• Different sized plastic bottles or large plastic jars filled 3/4 full with uncooked rice, sand, salt, lentils, peas or macaroni. Add a variety of plastic minibeasts • Magnifying glasses • Pictures/photos/name labels of minibeasts	Look carefully inside the bottle by rotating it so that the minibeasts are revealed for them to identify. Describe each minibeast they spot orally or in writing. Match the minibeast to a label with initial sounds and/or words.	• Fill balloons with minibeasts that are magnetic. Use magnets to move the minibeasts around inside the balloons. Can they guess the minibeast as they move them around the balloon using the magnet?

Select From the Following Suggested Focused Learning Possibilities

Communication & Language Listening & Attention	Literacy Reading	Literacy Writing
Use this challenge to: Provide opportunities for your children to practice listening to and follow a set of instructions.	**Use this challenge to:** Provide opportunities for your children to practice and apply their phonic knowledge of initial sounds and segmenting and blending.	**Use this challenge to:** Provide opportunities for your children to record what they see in the bottle in pictures, words and descriptive phrases.
I am learning to… • follow simple instructions (30-50) • concentrate until an activity is completed (40-60) • listen and respond to more complex instructions (ELG)	**I am learning to…** • recognise that some words start with the same sound (30-50) • hear and say initial sounds in words (40-60) • use my phonic knowledge to decode words (ELG)	**I am learning to…** • notice the difference between the marks that I make (22-36) • comment on the marks that I make (30-50) • write the sounds in simple words (40-60)
Challenge your children to: Give each other instructions to draw a minibeast that they have spotted inside the bottle e.g. draw an oval body, draw 8 legs.	**Challenge your children to:** Read description cards to help them identify the minibeast inside the bottle.	**Challenge your children to:** Use alliteration to describe their minibeasts e.g. creepy, crawly, curly caterpillar.

Characteristics of Effective Learning:

Motivation: I am learning to notice things in more detail
Motivation: I am learning to concentrate
Thinking: I am learning to reflect on how I have tackled a task and how well it is going

Maths Opportunities for using vocabulary and applying skills

Invite your children to:
- Count the minibeasts inside the bottle
- Estimate how many minibeasts they think there might be inside the bottle

Enhancing Provision Through Minibeasts

MINIBEAST RHYME

I'm a hairy spider, watch me spin,
I make silk webs to catch my food in.
I spin all day and I spin all night,
See my webs what a beautiful sight!

I'm a tiny ladybird, black and red,
I have two antennae on my head.
I spread my wings and start to fly,
Catching insects in the sky.

I'm a hairy caterpillar, sitting on a leaf,
Munching away without any teeth.
I'll eat and I'll grow...how big am I?
My chrysalis opens......I"m a butterfly!

With a house on my back, I'm a creepy crawly snail,
As I move very slowly I leave a sticky trail.
My shell is hard and sometimes I live inside,
So when the birds come along I have somewhere to hide.

I'm a wiggly worm, who lives underground,
If you dig in the soil then I'm sure to be found.
Sometimes I'm long and sometimes I'm short,
I stay underground in case I'm caught!

Ginny Morris

Challenge: **Malleable Minibeasts** Suggested Area of Provision: **Investigation**

Enhance with:	Invite your children to:	Other possible enhancements:
• Different coloured playdough, or clay, or pastry or florist oasis • Googly eyes Pebbles • Shells Matchsticks • Conkers Material • Buttons Pipe cleaners • Scissors Decorative Straws • Examples of minibeasts (photos, models)	Experiment with different ways of making their own minibeast encouraging them to think about the key features and the details they need to add.	• Make a minibeast out of food. • Add a large tray/container, a selection of fruit and vegetables and invite your children to make a healthy minibeast. • Add pasta of different shapes and colours to create minibeasts.

Select From the Following Suggested Focused Learning Possibilities

Communication & Language Speaking	Physical Development Moving & Handling	Understanding the World The World
Use this challenge to: Provide opportunities for your children to develop talk e.g. extending vocabulary, sentence structure, expressing thoughts and ideas.	**Use this challenge to:** Provide opportunities for your children to develop fine motor control over tools and malleable materials.	**Use this challenge to:** Provide opportunities for your children to practice, rehearse and apply their knowledge of minibeasts.
I am learning to… • talk in simple sentences (22-36) • retell something that happened in the right order (30-50) • talk about my ideas (40-60)	**I am learning to…** • control small equipment (22-36) • use one handed tools (30-50) • control and manipulate different tools safely (40-60)	**I am learning to…** • notice and talk about some of the things in my environment (22-36) • ask questions and talk about the world around me (30-50) • notice and talk about similarities and differences (40-60)
Challenge your children to: Use descriptive vocabulary to talk about their minibeast.	**Challenge your children to:** Add finer detail to their minibeast using tools e.g. can they make their spider hairy using a comb?	**Challenge your children to:** Make different types of minibeasts and talk about how and why they are similar/different.

Characteristics of Effective Learning:

Engagement: I am learning to use resources in unique and interesting ways
Motivation: I am learning to notice things in more detail
Thinking: I am learning to think of my own ideas

Mark Making/Writing Opportunities

Invite your children to:
- Draw and label their own model
- Draw a plan before making a minibeast

Maths Opportunities for using vocabulary and applying skills

Invite your children to:
- Measure the minibeast they have made
- Notice and create patterns on their minibeast

Enhancing Provision Through Minibeasts

Minibeast detectives
RSPCA

Challenge: **Create a 3D web**   Suggested Area of Provision: **Creative Workshop**

Enhance with:	Invite your children to:	Other enhancements:
- Paper plates - Hole punches - String - Wool - Ribbon - Laces - Thin strips of material - One hole hand punch - Pictures of webs	Punch holes around the edge of the paper plate and then encourage children to thread in and out of the holes to create a web.	- Add circular frames of different sizes e.g. hola hoop, sewing hoop. Attach string from one side to the other to create a star shape. Weave to create a web. - Provide boxes with an open side, put holes down each side and then weave from one side to the other. - Build a web outside using plastic tent pegs, mallets and string. - Knock nails or golf tees into a melon or pumpkin. Attach elastic bands, wool or string to make a web.

Select From the Following Suggested Focused Learning Possibilities

Physical Development Moving & Handling	Expressive Arts & Design Being Imaginative
Use this challenge to: Provide opportunities for your children to develop upper body strength and fine motor control in readiness for writing.	**Use this challenge to:** Provide opportunities for your children to develop ideas and experiences into their own representations.
I am learning to… - control small equipment (22-36) - use one-handed tools (30-50) - retrace over vertical lines (40-60)	**I am learning to…** - talk in simple terms about the 2D or 3D representations that I make (22-36) - create simple representations (40-60) - talk about the ideas and processes I have used (ELG)
	Challenge your children to: - Think of different ways to make holes in their paper plate. - Think of other ways to create a 3D web.

Characteristics of Effective Learning:

Engagement: I am learning to use resources in unique and interesting ways
Motivation: I am learning to notice things in more detail
Thinking: I am learning to think of my own ideas

Maths Opportunities for using vocabulary and applying skills

Invite your children to:
- Count the holes around the edge of the plate
- Use prepositional language as they talk about weaving in, out, through, over etc
- Compare the lengths of the resources they choose to weave

Enhancing Provision Through Minibeasts

CLOUD DOUGH
An Alternative to Play Dough

Ingredients

- 6 cups flour
- 2 cups chocolate powder
- 1 cup vegetable oil or baby oil
- Essential oil such as lavender or grapefruit (optional)

Steps

1. Pour the flour and chocolate powder into a large bowl.
2. Create a crater in the middle of the flour.
3. Pour the oil into the crater.
4. Gently mix it all together.
5. Enjoy mixing and learning about the properties of the dough

Challenge: **Digging for Worms**　　　　　Suggested Area of Provision: **Investigation**

Enhance the sand tray with:	Invite your children to:	Other possible enhancements:
• Compost • Cooked spaghetti or noodles or tagliatelle to use as 'worms' • Tweezers • Chopsticks • Pegs • Containers to collect worms • Scissors (can they pick up their 'worm' without cutting it!)	Choose tools to remove the pasta 'worms' from the compost. Encourage them to compare the lengths and textures of the 'worms'.	• Add other materials instead of compost e.g. sawdust, sand, cloud dough. • Colour spaghetti to add interest and compare similarities and differences. • Put in raw and cooked spaghetti so they can compare similarities and differences. • Add string, pipe cleaners, straws, jelly worms to be the 'worms' instead of pasta.

Select From the Following Suggested Focused Learning Possibilities

Communication & Language – Speaking	Physical Development – Moving & Handling	Understanding the World – The World
Use this challenge to: Provide opportunities for your children to develop descriptive vocabulary and talk in detail about their discoveries.	**Use this challenge to:** Provide opportunities for your children to develop strength in fingers and wrists to support a pincer and tripod grip.	**Use this challenge to:** Provide opportunities for your children to notice and talk about what they see and feel.
I am learning to… • use new words in my talking (22-36) • explain what is happening (30-50) • talk clearly about what I am thinking (40-60)	**I am learning to…** • control small equipment (22-36) • use one handed tools (30-50) • control and manipulate different tools safely (40-60)	**I am learning to…** • notice and talk about some of the things in my environment (22-36) • ask questions and talk about the world around me (30-50) • notice and talk about similarities and differences (40-60)
		Challenge your children to: • Look for real worms in the environment and talk about their key features using the correct vocabulary.

Characteristics of Effective Learning:

Engagement: I am learning to investigate
Motivation: I am learning to try different ways of doing things when one approach doesn't work
Thinking: I am learning to change my strategy when necessary

Mark Making/Writing Opportunities

Invite your children to:
• Record the measurements of their 'worms'

Maths Opportunities for using vocabulary and applying skills

Invite your children to:
• Estimate and compare the different lengths of worms that they find

Enhancing Provision Through Minibeasts

Incy Wincy spider

Climbed up the water spout.

Down came the rain and washed the spider out!

Out came the sunshine and dried up all the rain,

So Incy Wincy spider climbed up the spout again!

Incy Wincy spider

Sat on a fallen twig

Down came the rain with raindrops wet and big!

Incy ran away to find a place to dry,

And when the rain had gone he had another try!

Incy Wincy spider

Crossed the icy lane.

Out came the sunshine and Incy was in trouble again!

He tried to keep his balance but his feet were frozen too

So Incy quickly spun a web and disappeared from view!

Ginny Morris

Challenge: **Wash the Spider Down the Spout!**   Suggested Area of Provision: **Investigation**

Enhance the water tray with:	Invite your children to:	Other possible enhancements:

• Different sized plastic guttering
• Plastic tubes
• Funnels
• Different sized plastic spiders
• Different sized pouring equipment e.g. jugs, beakers, egg cups, spoons, ladles
• Timers
• Laminated copies of the Incy Wincy Spider nursery rhyme
	Experiment by filling containers with water pouring the water down the 'spout'. Can they wash the spider into the water tray?
	
	Challenge the children to find out:
	• How long it takes for the spider to get to the bottom of the spout
	• How many containers of water it takes
	• How they might catch the spider at the bottom
		• Swop the guttering and tubes for:
		    - Ice
		    - Planks of wood
		    - Branches or twigs

Select From the Following Suggested Focused Learning Possibilities

Communication & Language Understanding	Physical Development Moving & Handling	Mathematics Shape, Space & Measure
Use this challenge to: Provide opportunities for your children to develop their ability to ask and answer questions.	**Use this challenge to:** Provide opportunities for your children to develop upper body strength and bilateral co-ordination (using 2 hands together) in readiness for writing.	**Use this challenge to:** Provide opportunities for your children to practice and rehearse mathematical vocabulary about length, time and capacity.
I am learning to… • answer who, what, where questions (22-36) • understand simple concepts (22-36) • answer how and why questions about my experiences (ELG)	**I am learning to…** • control small equipment (22-36) • use one handed tools (30-50) • use two hands together (40-60)	**I am learning to…** • use language of size (22-36) • use the correct vocabulary to talk about size, capacity and time (ELG)
		Challenge your children to: Select and use timers to measure how long it takes for the spider to reach the bottom of the tube.

Characteristics of Effective Learning:

Motivation: I am learning to try different ways of doing things when one approach doesn't work

Thinking: I am learning to talk about problems I encounter and find ways to solve them

Mark Making/Writing Opportunities

Invite your children to:
- Record how fast the spider went down
- Make up their own Incy Wincy rhyme

Enhancing Provision Through Minibeasts

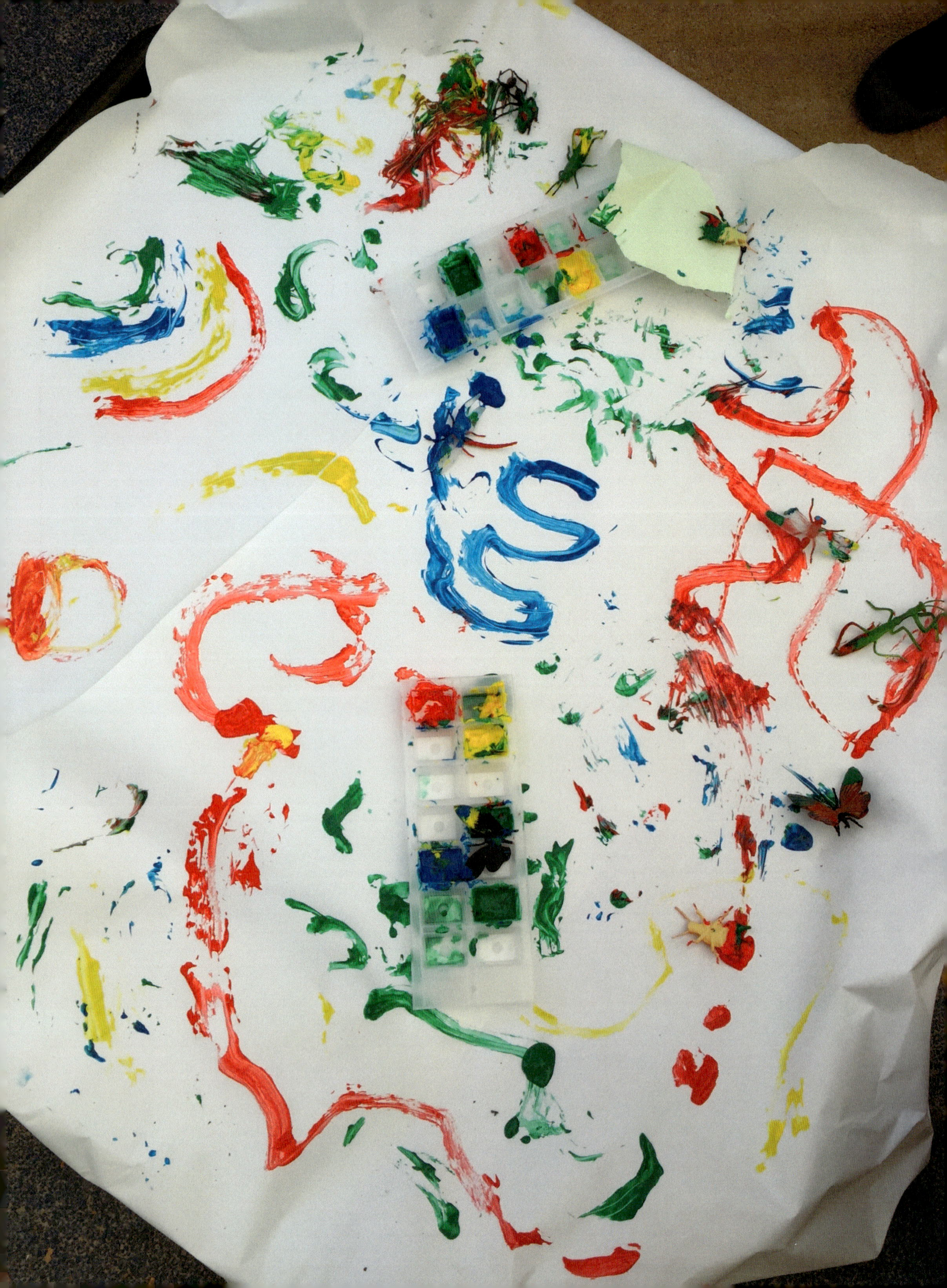

Challenge: Sensory Painting   Suggested Area of Provision: **Creative Workshop**

Enhance with:	Invite your children to:	Other possible enhancements:
• Frozen minibeasts (Put plastic mini beasts in ice-cube trays, fill with different coloured paint and freeze) • Large paper	Move the frozen minibeasts around the paper to create pictures and patterns. Can they identify the minibeast as the paint begins to melt?	• Experiment freezing minibeasts in other substances e.g. chocolate, shampoo, different coloured fruit juices, yogurt, gravy, jelly. • Instead of paper, paint on perspex or mirrors or tin foil. What different effects can they create? • Create a map or trail for the children to follow with the frozen minibeasts.

Select From the Following Suggested Focused Learning Possibilities

Communication & Language Speaking	Understanding the World The World	Expressive Arts & Design Exploring Media & Materials
Use this challenge to: Provide opportunities for your children to narrate and describe what they are seeing, doing and creating.	**Use this challenge to:** Provide opportunities for your children to observe, explain and describe the properties of frozen materials and how they change over time.	**Use this challenge to:** Provide opportunities for your children to express their imagination and represent their ideas in original ways.
I am learning to… • use new words in my talking (22-36) • explain what is happening (30-50) • talk about my ideas (40-60)	**I am learning to…** • talk about why things happen (30-50) • notice and talk about changes that take place over time (40-60) • describe the properties of different materials (ELG)	**I am learning to…** • talk in simple terms about the 2D representations that I make (22-36) • create simple representations (40-60) • use media and materials in original ways (ELG)
Challenge your children to: Add more information and detail to describe what they are seeing and feeling.	**Challenge your children to:** Think of other materials and substances that can be changed in different ways e.g. boiling water into steam, melting candle wax, burning paper.	**Challenge your children to:** Think about imaginative ways to use the frozen minibeasts with different media e.g. painting with them on wood, the playground or chalkboards.

Characteristics of Effective Learning:

Engagement: I am learning to try new things
Motivation: I am learning to choose the things that really fascinate me
Thinking: I am learning to predict

SNAIL FACTS

- I hibernate during the winter and live off my body fat.

- I only have one foot.

- I cannot see very well so find food through touch and smell.

- I can crawl upside down.

- I don't always move in straight lines, sometimes I move in a circle.

- I can live up to 15 years.

- I have tentacles, 2 are for eyes and 2 for feeling.

- I am nocturnal and more active at night.

- I produce thick slime which protects me from getting hurt.

- Some people like to eat me!

- Some gardeners don't like me because I eat garden plants and vegetables.

- If it is too dry I hide in my shell for months.

- I carry a shell on my back.

Challenge: **Snail Slime** Suggested Area of Provision: **Outdoors**

Enhance with:	Invite your children to:	Other possible enhancements:
• Empty plastic washing up liquid bottles • Washing up liquid • Honey • Thick paint	Choose a liquid to fill their bottle e.g. washing up liquid, honey or paint and encourage them to squeeze it out onto paper or other surfaces outside, to create their own slime trail. How long a trail can they make with one squeeze?	• Add other liquids for children to experiment with e.g. gloop, custard, runny icing sugar.

Select From the Following Suggested Focused Learning Possibilities

Physical Development Moving & Handling	Mathematics Shape, Space & Measure	Expressive Arts & Design Using Media & Materials
Use this challenge to: Provide opportunities for your children to develop strength and stamina in fine and gross motor skills.	**Use this challenge to:** Provide opportunities for your children to talk about size, length and position.	**Use this challenge to:** Provide opportunities for your children to investigate the properties of different materials.
I am learning to… • develop finger strength (22-36) • draw lines and circles (30-50) • control small apparatus (40-60)	**I am learning to…** • use language of size (22-36) • use positional words (30-50) • order objects by length (40-60)	**I am learning to…** • experiment with different media and materials (22-36) • talk about how different things feel (30-50) • that different media creates different effects (40-60)
Challenge your children to: Use thicker substances in the bottles encouraging them to use more strength to create a trail.	**Challenge your children to:** Use non-standard/standard units of measure to find out how long their slime trail is. Who has made the longest/shortest trail?	

Characteristics of Effective Learning:

Engagement: I am learning to pretend that objects are something else
Motivation: I am learning to try different ways of doing things when one approach doesn't work
Thinking: I am learning to set hypotheses and test out my ideas

Mark Making/Writing Opportunities

Invite your children to:
• Record their measurements
• Create lines, shapes, patterns and pictures with their snail slime

SPIDER STEPS

A black hairy spider,
Crawled across the wall.
Counting out his footsteps,
As he tried not to fall!

1 step, 2 steps,
3 steps, 4.
On and on and on he goes,
Oops… he is on the floor!

5 steps, 6 steps,
7 steps, 8.
Shhh… he hears the hoover,
Be still and just wait!

9 steps, 10 steps,
A dark secret den.
Spin your sticky web spider,
Before we count back from 10!

10,9,8,7,6,5,4,3,2,1,0

Ginny Morris

| Challenge: **Spider Games** | | Suggested Area of Provision: **Maths Area** |

Enhance with:	Invite your children to:	Other possible enhancements:
• Different sized dice or spinners with numbers/spots appropriate to your children • Plastic spiders or spiders that children have made themselves • A large drawn spiders' web • Whiteboards and pens for recording	Think of their own spider game using a drawn web, spiders and dice/spinners e.g. throw the dice and move spiders onto the web to see who can reach the centre first.	• Put shapes on the dice instead of numbers and play a shape game. • Add numbers to the web so children can match numbers. • Add paper on clipboards to tally totals, practice number formation and calculation.

Select From the Following Suggested Focused Learning Possibilities

Personal, Social & Emotional Development Making Relationships	Mathematics Number	
Use this challenge to: Provide opportunities for your children to share and take turns.	**Use this challenge to:** Provide opportunities for your children to practice and apply number skills and mathematical language.	
I am learning to… • join in with others during my play (22-36) • talk to others in my play (30-50) • explain what I know and understand (40-60)	**I am learning to…** • say some number names in sequence (22-36) • match numerals with an amount of objects (30-50) • use the right mathematical language (40-60)	
Challenge your children to: Devise their own rules for their game by discussing and sharing ideas.	**Challenge your children to:** Work out one more/one less than the number on the dice. Use 2 dice to practice addition and subtraction.	

Characteristics of Effective Learning:

Engagement: I am learning to combine resources in my play
Motivation: I am learning to try different ways of doing things when one approach doesn't work
Thinking: I am learning to reflect on how I have tackled a task and how well it is going

Mark Making/Writing Opportunities

Invite your children to:
• Record their own scores
• Write a list of players
• Practise number formation
• Write a set of rules for their game

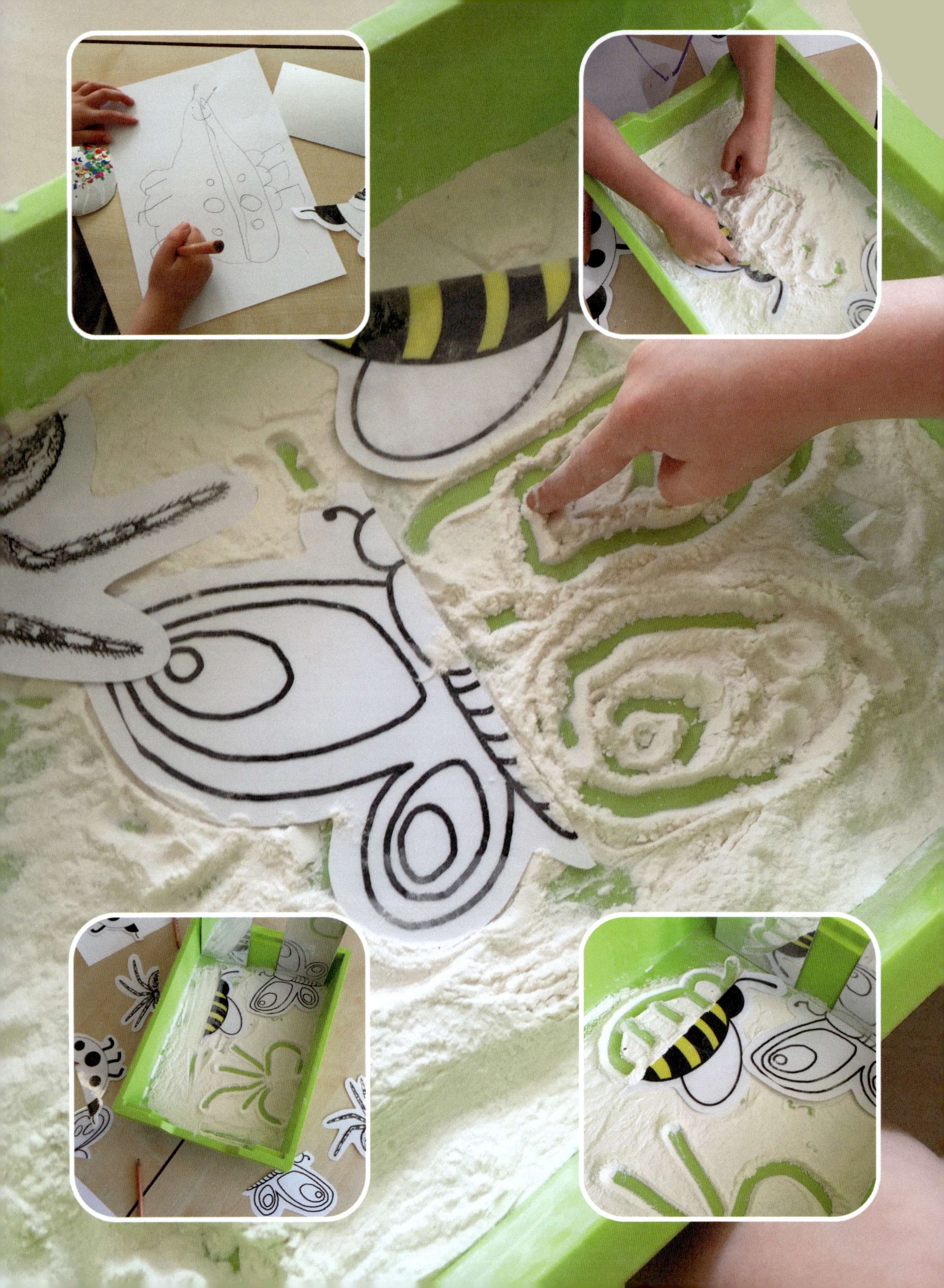

Challenge: **Symmetrical Minibeasts** Suggested Area of Provision: **Writing Area**

Enhance with:	Invite your children to:	Other possible enhancements:
- Trays filled with flour or icing sugar or glitter or shaving foam. Add mirrors around the edge of the tray to reflect the symmetry - Examples of half drawn minibeasts on card - Plain paper and writing tools to draw their own symmetrical patterns	Draw half of a minibeast with their fingers using the half shapes and mirrors to help them.	- Add other tools e.g chopsticks, cocktail sticks, stirrers, paint brushes to use instead of fingers. - Add decoration to add to their minibeast e.g. sequins, beads, buttons.

Select From the Following Suggested Focused Learning Possibilities

Physical Development Moving & Handling	Mathematics Shape, Space & Measure	Expressive Arts & Design Using Media & Materials
Use this challenge to: Provide opportunities for your children to practise dexterity and control in finger movements when using one handed tools.	**Use this challenge to:** Provide opportunities for your children to talk about, describe and draw different shapes and patterns.	**Use this challenge to:** Provide opportunities for your children to develop, extend and review their ideas and thinking.
I am learning to… - draw lines and circles (30-50) - retrace vertical lines and use anti-clockwise movements (40-60) - handle equipment and tools with dexterity (ELG)	**I am learning to…** - notice simple shapes and patterns (22-36) - use shapes appropriately in my play (30-50) - use shapes to create patterns (40-60)	**I am learning to…** - use lines to create shapes and objects (30-50) - review my work and change it if I need to (40-60) - extend and develop my ideas (ELG)
Challenge your children to: Use writing tools with the correct tripod grip to draw the shapes.	**Challenge your children to:** Notice and talk about halves of shapes and symmetry.	**Challenge your children to:** Think of a different way to produce a symmetrical picture.

Characteristics of Effective Learning:

Engagement: I am learning how making mistakes can help me with my learning

Motivation: I am learning to notice things in more detail

Thinking: I am learning to recognise when my previous learning or experiences link to what I am doing

Enhancing Provision Through Minibeasts

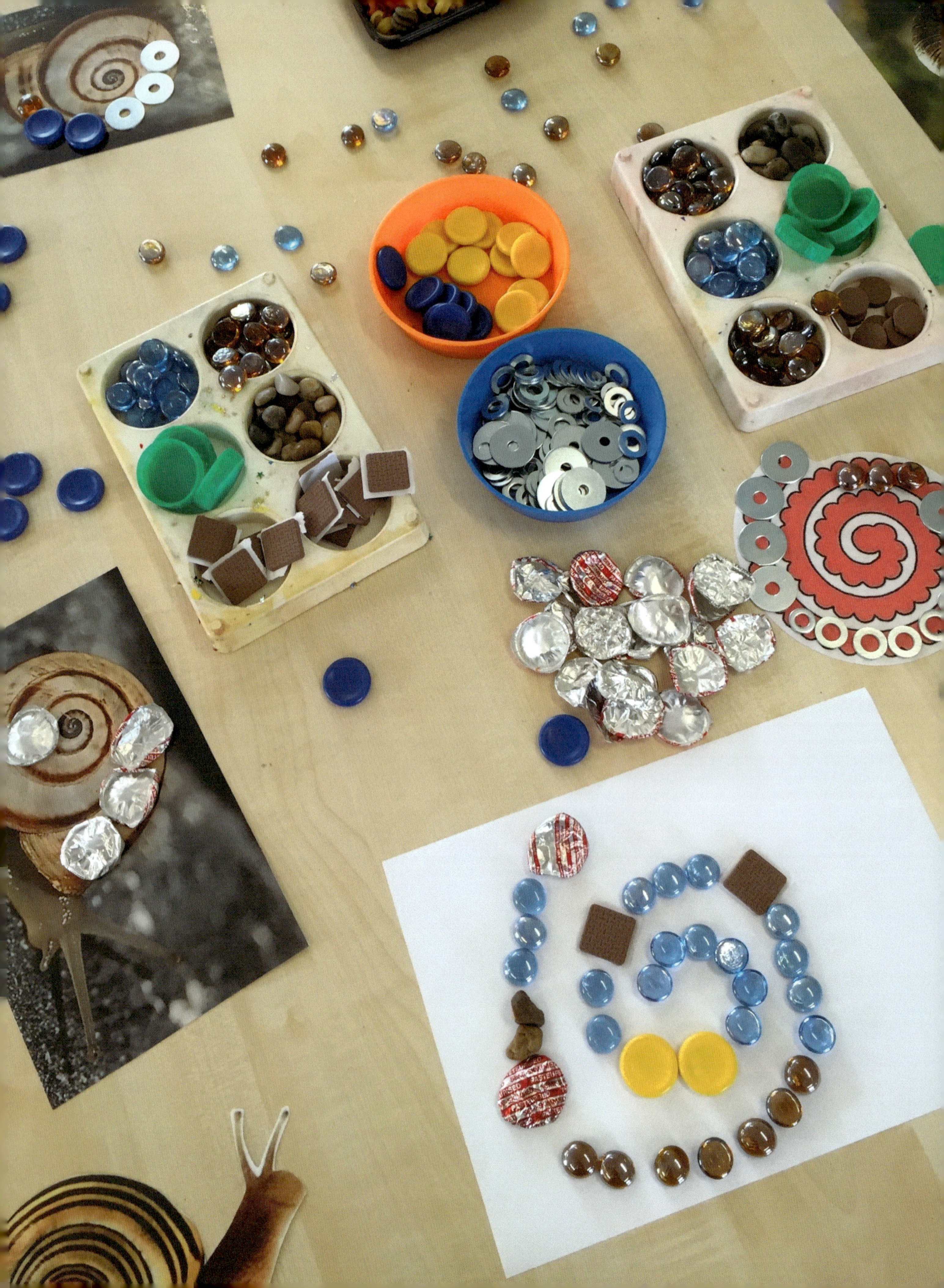

Challenge: **Spiral Patterns** Suggested Area of Provision: **Creative Workshop**

Enhance with:	Invite your children to:	Other possible enhancements:
• Items for placing e.g. stones, beads, buttons, pasta shapes, bottle tops, conkers, petals, leaves, shells • Simple spiral patterns drawn on paper • Paper or card of different colours	Choose and then place their own resources to create their own spiral shapes and patterns.	• Use different surfaces to place the spiral patterns on e.g. mirrors or perspex, squares of flat wood, foil trays.

Select From the Following Suggested Focused Learning Possibilities

Mathematics Shape, Space & Measure	Expressive Arts & Design Using Media & Materials	
Use this challenge to: Provide opportunities for your children to learn and practise mathematical vocabulary to describe shapes and patterns.	**Use this challenge to:** Provide opportunities for your children to develop their own ideas making independent decisions and choices.	
I am learning to… • notice simple shapes and patterns (22-36) • use shapes in my play (30-50) • use shape to create patterns (40-60)	**I am learning to…** • experiment with different materials and media (22-36) • use lines to create shapes and objects (30-50) • extend and develop my ideas (ELG)	
Challenge your children to: Place objects to represent more complex shapes e.g. isosceles triangle, trapezium.	**Challenge your children to:** Work in groups outside to create larger spiral shapes using natural materials.	

Characteristics of Effective Learning:

Engagement: I am learning to combine resources in my play
Thinking: I am learning to make decisions

Mark Making/Writing Opportunities

Invite your children to:
- Draw their own spiral shapes and use them to place different materials on top
- Trace spiral shapes in e.g. paint, sand, glitter using fingers and simple tools e.g. paintbrushes, lolly sticks etc

Enhancing Provision Through Minibeasts

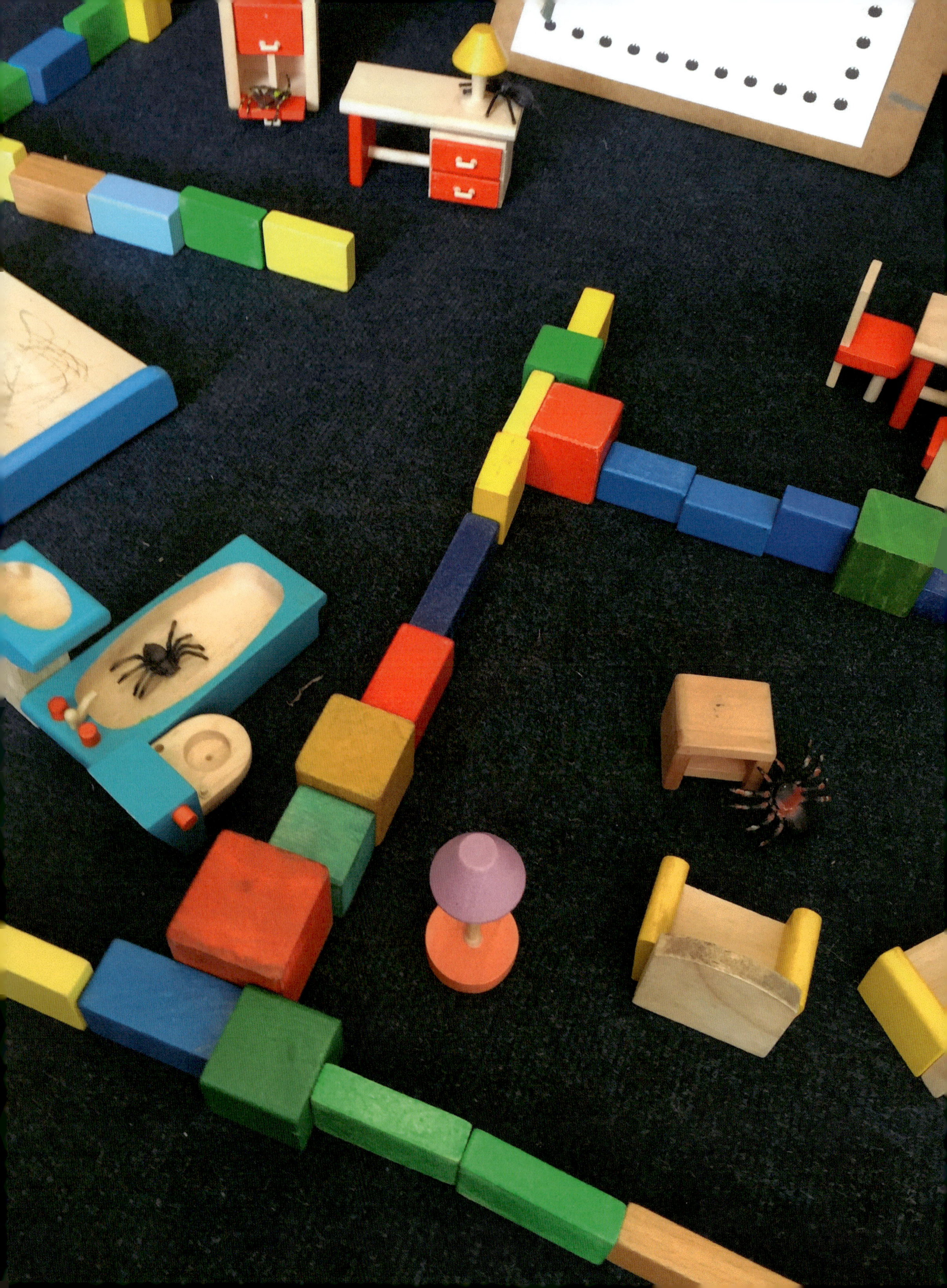

Challenge: **Spider Adventures**   Suggested Area of Provision: **Small World & Construction**

Enhance with:	Invite your children to:	Other possible enhancements:
• A house scene using small world furniture and construction equipment • Plastic spiders and story books about spiders • A variety of note books, spider and web shaped paper	Hide the spiders in the small world scene and then encourage the children to make up an oral or written story about what happens to the spider.	• Create an outdoor scene using a tuft spot and spiders. • Hide spiders in intriguing and unusual places for children to find as a stimulus to create stories.

Select From the Following Suggested Focused Learning Possibilities

Communication & Language Speaking	Personal, Social & Emotional Development Managing Feelings & Behaviour	
Use this challenge to: Provide opportunities for your children to practice oral story telling.	**Use this challenge to:** Provide opportunities for your children to develop their understanding of their own and others feelings and behaviour.	
I am learning to… • use word endings (22-36) • use different tenses in my talk (30-50) • tell stories orally (40-60)	**I am learning to…** • show how I feel (22-36) • that my actions and words can affect others (30-50) • talk about my own and others' feelings (40-60)	
Challenge your children to: • Add descriptive detail to their oral narrative. • Order their ideas in the correct sequence using time words e.g. first, next, in the beginning, finally.	**Challenge your children to:** Talk about and share their own experiences, likes, dislikes and fears about spiders.	

Characteristics of Effective Learning:

Engagement: I am learning to act out my experiences in my play
Motivation: I am learning to concentrate
Thinking: I am learning to recognise when my previous learning or experiences link to what I am doing

Mark Making/Writing Opportunities

Invite your children to:
• Order their ideas in the correct sequence using time words e.g. first, next, in the beginning, finally
• Record their stories in written form
• Add descriptive detail to their written narrative

Maths Opportunities for using vocabulary and applying skills

Invite your children to:
• Use prepositional language to describe where their spiders are

Enhancing Provision Through Minibeasts

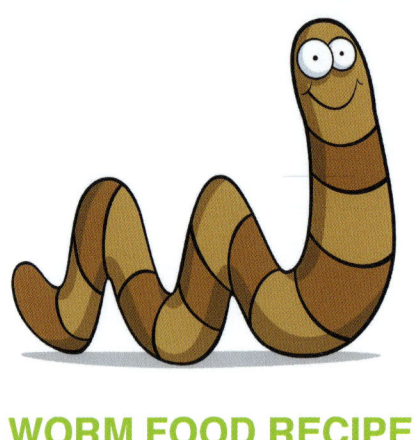

WORM FOOD RECIPE

Ingredients

- 1 cup of sawdust
- 4 large leaves
- 1 spoon of grass
- Peel from an apple or orange or pear
- 2 cups of soil
- 3 cups of water

Instructions

1. Mash up the leaves and grass
2. Cut up the peel into small pieces and add to the leaves and grass
3. Mix the sawdust and the soil together
4. Mix all the dry ingredients together
5. Add the water and stir well

Challenge: Feed the Worms   Suggested Area of Provision: **Investigation**

Enhance the mud kitchen with:	Invite your children to:	
• Leaves • Twigs • Fruit peel • Grass cuttings • Flower petals • Seeds • Rolling pins • Pestle & mortar • Example recipes	Choose from a selection of natural materials and combine these by chopping, grinding and mixing to create their own worm food.	

Select From the Following Suggested Focused Learning Possibilities

Personal, Social & Emotional Development Self-confidence & self-awareness	Expressive Arts & Design Using Media & Materials
Use this challenge to: Provide opportunities for your children to make independent choices and decisions.	**Use this challenge to:** Provide opportunities for your children to explore different materials and express their ideas.
I am learning to… • show others what I like and what interests me (22-36) • choose activities and resources with help (30-50) • talk to other people about what I'm interested in and what I think (40-60)	**I am learning to…** • experiment with different materials and media (22-36) • talk about how different things feel (30-50) • choose the correct resources for the job (40-60)

Characteristics of Effective Learning:

Engagement: I am learning to try new things
Motivation: I am learning to choose the things that really fascinate me
Thinking: I am learning to make decisions

Mark Making/Writing Opportunities

Invite your children to…
• Make their own recipe book for different minibeasts

Maths Opportunities for using vocabulary and applying skills

Invite your children to:
• Use weighing equipment e.g. weighing scales to measure their ingredients
• Solve number problems to make their recipe for 1, 2, 3 or more worms

Enhancing Provision Through Minibeasts

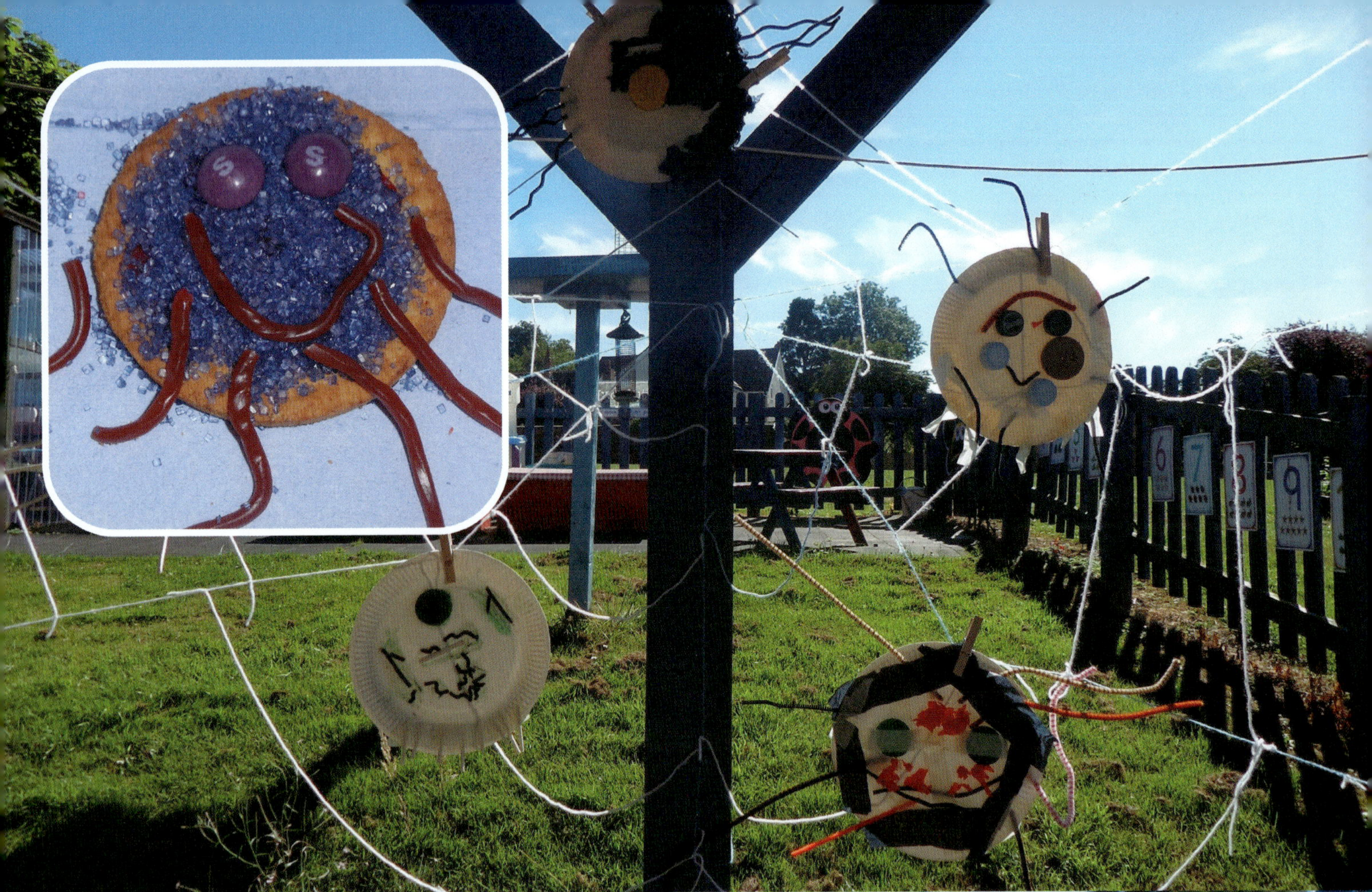

6
7
8
9

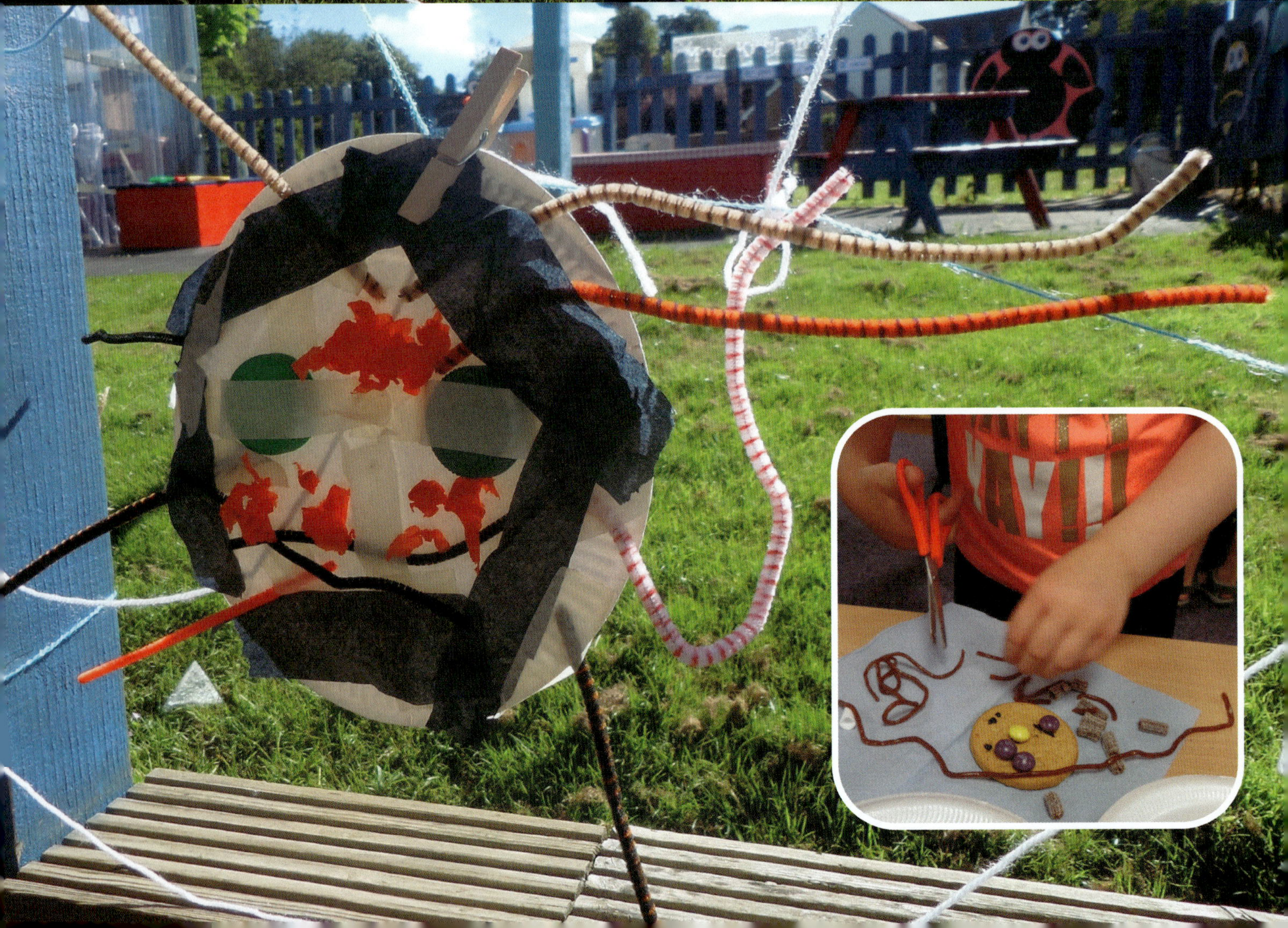

Challenge: **Thread a Minibeast** Suggested Area of Provision: **Finger Gym**

Enhance with:	Invite your children to:	Other possible enhancements:
- Pipe cleaners - Laces - Uncooked pasta - Beads - Silver milk bottle tops - Plastic bottle tops with holes - Off cuts of wood	Choose from a variety of objects that can be threaded to create their own minibeast.	- Thread an edible minibeast using e.g. strawberry laces, cheese strings, Hola Hoops, Polos, Cheerios.

Select From the Following Suggested Focused Learning Possibilities

Physical Development — Moving & Handling	Mathematics — Number
Use this challenge to: Provide opportunities for your children to practise and refine hand-eye co-ordination, finger movements and using two hands together in readiness for writing.	**Use this challenge to:** Provide opportunities for your children to apply their number skills to estimate, count and compare quantities.
I am learning to… - manipulate small objects (22-36) - use a pincer grip (30-50) - use two hands together (40-60)	**I am learning to…** - talk about quantities (22-36) - to identify when two sets of objects have the same amount in them (30-50) - estimate (40-60)
Challenge your children to: Use thinner and smaller resources for children to create their own minibeast.	**Challenge your children to:** Talk about calculation using vocabulary of more/less/altogether/total etc.

Characteristics of Effective Learning:

Engagement: I am learning to tackle things that may be difficult
Motivation: I am learning to be resilient when things get difficult
Thinking: I am learning to talk about the problems I encounter and find ways to solve them

Mark Making/Writing Opportunities

Invite your children to:
- Make representative drawings of their minibeast and label them

Enhancing Provision Through Minibeasts

WORM FACTS

- I do not have hands or feet or teeth or a tongue.

- I breathe through my skin but I don't have lungs.

- I am covered in hairs or bristles to help me move.

- The fat pink part of me is called my 'saddle'.

- My body is divided into segments.

- I have only got three senses, taste, smell and touch.

- I eat leaves, rotting vegetation, soil and minerals.

- I eat my own weight in food everyday.

- If you cut me in half, only half of my body will die.

- I like dark places and burrow tunnels.

- I need to be in a wet place to survive.

- To survive in winter I burrow deep into the soil.

- I eat my way through soil and then poo it out behind me.

Challenge: **Magnetic Minibeasts** Suggested Area of Provision: **Maths Area**

Enhance with:	Invite your children to:	Other possible enhancements:
• Trays filled with shredded green and brown paper • Magnetic minibeasts (or pictures with paperclips) • Magnets • Containers to collect the minibeasts	Use the magnets to rescue as many minibeasts as they can from the tray.	• Add other objects that are not magnetic to encourage problem solving. • Add timers to encourage discussion about how long it takes to rescue all the minibeasts. • Add number lines to help children count and compare amounts of mnibeasts that they have rescued.

Select From the Following Suggested Focused Learning Possibilities

Communication & Language Speaking	Mathematics Number
Use this challenge to: Provide opportunities for your children to ask questions and develop explanations.	**Use this challenge to:** Provide opportunities for your children to practise and apply number skills in counting and calculation.
I am learning to… • ask 'what', 'who', 'where' questions (22-36) • explain what is happening (30-50) • talk clearly about what I am thinking (40-60)	**I am learning to…** • talk about quantities (22-36) • count a group of objects (30-50) • find 1 more and 1 less (40-60)
Challenge your children to: Give detailed accounts and explanations about what is happening either factual about the magnets or through storytelling.	**Challenge your children to:** Talk about calculation using vocabulary of more/less/altogether/total etc.

Characteristics of Effective Learning:

Engagement: I am learning to investigate
Motivation: I am learning to concentrate
Thinking: I am learning to predict

Mark Making/Writing Opportunities

Invite your children to:
- Record how many minibeasts they rescue
- Draw pictures of the minibeasts they have rescued
- Label the minibeasts they have rescued

LADYBIRD FACTS

- Ladybirds are a type of beetle.

- Some Ladybirds have no spots, others have up to 20 spots.

- Ladybirds are red as a warning to their predators that they do not taste very nice!

- During the winter ladybirds hibernate together to stay warm.

- Ladybirds smell with their feet and antennae.

- A ladybird has 2 sets of wings. The outer set is a hard shell for protection and the inner set are what they use to fly.

- Female ladybirds are larger than male ladybirds.

- Ladybirds eat pests like greenfly so gardeners love them.

- The seven spotted ladybird is the most common.

Challenge: **Create a 2D Web** Suggested Area of Provision: **Mark-making**

Enhance with:	Invite your children to:	Other possible enhancements:
- Pictures and simple line drawings of webs - Shallow trays - Shaving foam	Look carefully at the pictures to help them draw lines to create the shape of a spider's web in the foam.	- Add glitter or coloured sand or lentils or cooked spaghetti or peppercorns or flour, or mixed herbs or gravy granuals instead of shaving foam. - Add tools e.g. brushes, chopsticks, straws, lolly sticks, pencils and challenge the children to use them to draw a web. How much detail can they add? - Add pencils, paper & rulers and challenge the children to draw their own intricate web. How similar to the pictures do their webs look? - Use larger equipment outside e.g. skipping ropes or ride bikes through paint onto large paper.

Select From the Following Suggested Focused Learning Possibilities

Physical Development Moving & Handling	Understanding the World The World	
Use this challenge to: Provide opportunities for your children to develop fine motor control in readiness for writing.	**Use this challenge to:** Provide opportunities for your children to develop skills in observing carefully and noticing detail.	
I am learning to… - draw simple shapes (22-36) - use anti-clockwise movements (40-60) - retrace over vertical lines (40-60) - handle equipment & tools with dexterity (ELG)	**I am learning to…** - notice and talk about some of the things in my immediate environment (22-36) - look carefully at the world around me (30-50) - notice and talk about patterns (40-60)	

Characteristics of Effective Learning:

Motivation: I am learning to notice things in more detail
Thinking: I am learning to talk about my thinking

Maths Opportunities for using vocabulary and applying skills

Invite your children to:
- Talk about the patterns they notice and create
- Identify the different shapes within their webs

Enhancing Provision Through Minibeasts

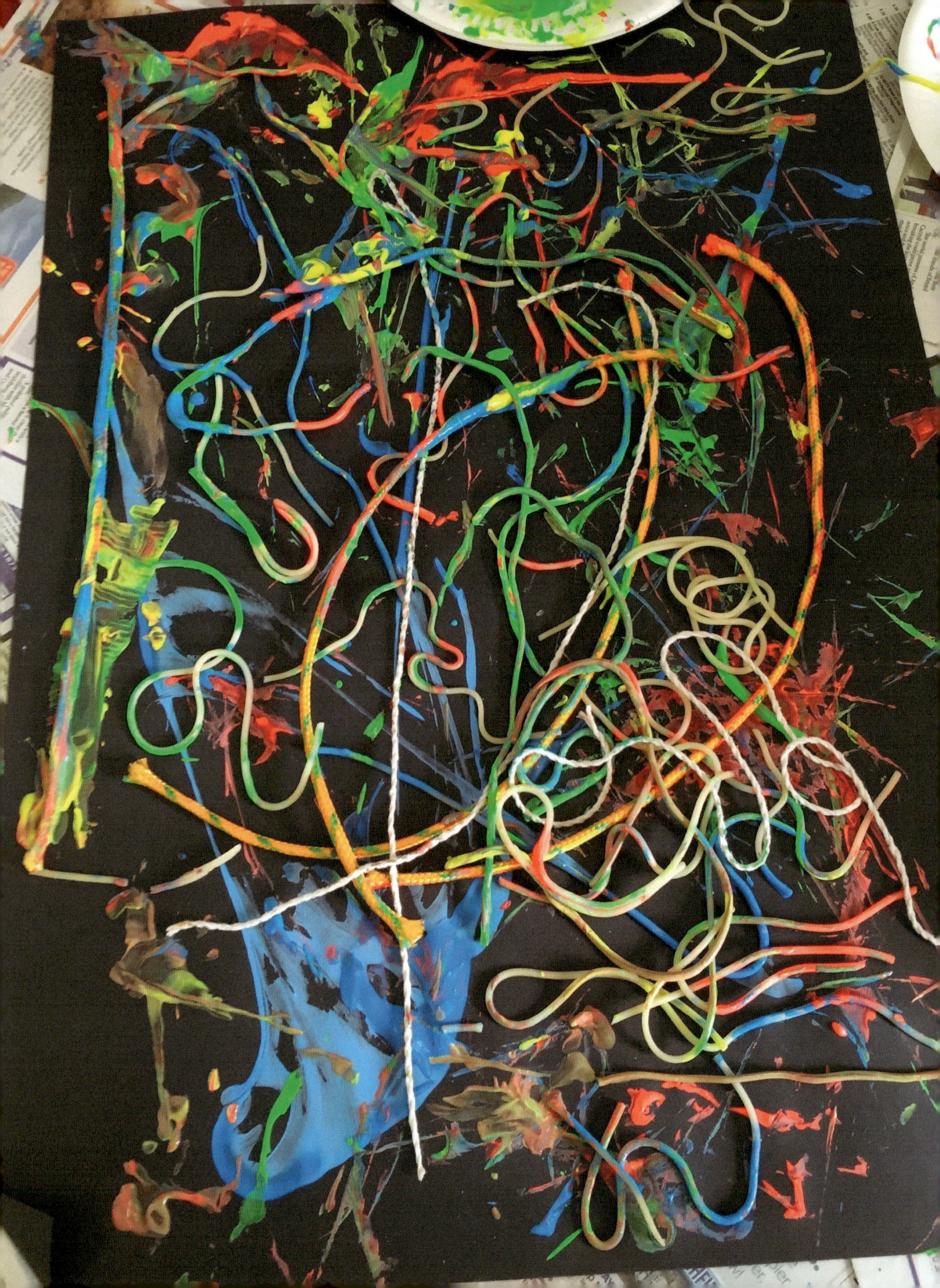

Challenge: **Worm Trails** Suggested Area of Provision: **Creative Workshop**

Enhance with:	Invite your children to:	Other possible enhancements:
- Cooked spaghetti - Wool - Thick string/rope - Different coloured paint	Create their own worm trail by dipping the spaghetti into the paint and wiggling the 'worms' around the paper to create a trail.	- Use pipe cleaners, laces, noodles, threaded beads, fingers. - Use larger equipment e.g. broom handles, flexible tubing, insulation tubing to create larger trails outside.

Select From the Following Suggested Focused Learning Possibilities

Physical Development Moving & Handling	Expressive Arts & Design Exploring Media & Materials	
Use this challenge to: Provide opportunities for your children to practise gross and fine motor control.	**Use this challenge to:** Provide opportunities for your children to explore how different materials can create different effects.	
I am learning to… - draw simple shapes (22-36) - draw lines and circles (30-50) - use anti-clockwise movements and retrace vertical lines (40-60)	**I am learning to…** - experiment with different materials and media (22-36) - use lines to create shapes (30-50) - that different media creates different effects (40-60)	
	Challenge your children to: Think about other ways to create worm trails on a large and small scale.	

Characteristics of Effective Learning:

Engagement: I am learning to try new things
Motivation: I am learning to choose the things that really fascinate me
Thinking: I am learning to find different ways to do things

Maths Opportunities for using vocabulary and applying skills

Invite your children to:
- Compare the different lengths of their worm trails
- Notice and talk about the patterns that they make with their trails
- Compare the different thicknesses of the materials that they use

Enhancing Provision Through Minibeasts

SPIDER FACTS

- I have 8 legs.

- My two body parts are called abdomen and thorax.

- I have 6 or 8 eyes.

- I have fangs.

- Some of us shed our skins which is called moulting.

- My family is called Arachnid.

- I eat small insects that are garden pests.

- Each day I make a new web and roll up the old one and eat it.

- I use the hair on my body to find my way around as my eyes do not see very far.

- If I lose a leg I grow a new one.

- The silk for my web comes from inside by body and I squeeze it out of two holes called spinnerets at the back of my body.

- Everyone in my family likes to live in dry places.

- Someone in my family is called a Tarantula.

- Birds, wasps, snakes, fish, lizards and frogs like to eat me.

Challenge: **Minibeast Maths** Suggested Area of Provision: **Maths Area**

Enhance with:	Invite your children to:	Other possible enhancements:
• A selection of jars of different sizes and shapes (or pictures of jars) • Dice or spinner • Plastic minibeasts • Clipboards or notepads to record scores	Play a game where they shake the dice and put the corresponding amount of minibeasts in their jar.	• Different coloured dice (one colour for adding to the jar and the other for taking away from the jar).

Select From the Following Suggested Focused Learning Possibilities

Personal, Social & Emotional Development Making Relationships	Mathematics Number
Use this challenge to: Provide opportunities for your children to develop co-operative play, turn taking and sharing ideas.	**Use this challenge to:** Provide opportunities for your children to practise and apply the skills of counting, estimating and calculation.
I am learning to… • join in with others in my play (22-36) • think of my own ideas in my play (30-50) • take turns (ELG)	**I am learning to…** • compare different quantities (22-36) • match numerals with an amount of objects (30-50) • count out objects from a large group (40-60)
Challenge your children to: Design a new game with rules for others to play.	**Challenge your children to:** • Estimate how many minbeasts are in their jar. • Use different coloured dice to practise adding and taking away e.g. black dice to add minbeasts to the jar and red dice to take minbeasts out of the jar.

Characteristics of Effective Learning:

Engagement: I am learning to tackle things that may be difficult
Motivation: I am learning to persist even when things get difficult
Thinking: I am learning to find different ways to do things

Mark Making/Writing Opportunities

Invite your children to:
• Find a way to record their calculations
• Record the rules of the game

WHAT AM I?

What am I? • I live in the earth. • I eat soil and poo it out behind me. • I need to be in a wet place to survive. • I have not got any legs.	**I am a worm.**
What am I? • I am red as a warning to others. • I can live for up to a year. • I have two sets of wings. • I have black spots.	**I am a ladybird.**
What am I? • I have six or eight eyes. • If I lose a leg I grow a new one. • All my family like to live in dry places. • Each day I make a new web.	**I am a spider.**
What am I? • I can taste with my feet. • I have colourful wings. • I like sweet juice to drink. • I start out as a caterpillar.	**I am a butterfly.**
What am I? • I can crawl upside down. • I have one foot. • I make thick slime so I don't get hurt. • I carry a shell on my back.	**I am a snail.**

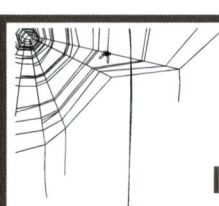

Enhancing Provision Through Minibeasts

Challenge: **Name the Minibeast** Suggested Area of Provision: **Small World**

Enhance with:	Invite your children to:	Other possible enhancements:
• A selection of different sized and coloured plastic bottle tops with initial sounds for each minibeast written on them • A variety of plastic minibeasts that will fit into the tops • Tweezers, pegs, chopsticks, tongs and other tools to pick up the minibeasts	Pick up a minibeast out of a container of mixed minibeasts using the tools provided and match it to the correct initial letter sound on one of the bottle tops.	• Add bottle tops with blank labels for children to write on. • Add short descriptive sentences about each minibeast to the bottle tops.

Select From the Following Suggested Focused Learning Possibilities

Physical Development — Moving and Handling	Literacy — Reading	
Use this challenge to: Provide opportunities for your children to practise hand-eye co-ordination, finger isolation and finger strength to support the development of the pincer and tripod grips.	**Use this challenge to:** Provide opportunities for your children to practise making the link between phonemes (sounds in words) and graphemes (the written symbol).	
I am learning to… • use one handed tools (30-50) • control and manipulate different tools safely (40-60) • handle equipment and tools with dexterity (ELG)	**I am learning to…** • recognise that some words start with the same sound (30-50) • which letter shapes represent sounds (40-60) • use my phonic knowledge to decode words (ELG)	
	Challenge your children to: Read simple sentences which give descriptions and clues about various minibeasts e.g. 'I have wings'.	

Characteristics of Effective Learning:

Engagement: I am learning when I practise things I can get better
Motivation: I am learning to concentrate
Thinking: I am learning to talk about my thinking

Mark Making/Writing Opportunities

Invite your children to:
• Write their own initial sounds or clues on the bottle tops

Maths Opportunities for using vocabulary and applying skills

Invite your children to:
• Count how many minibeasts start with the same initial sound
• Sort the minibeasts by their initial sound

Enhancing Provision Through Minibeasts

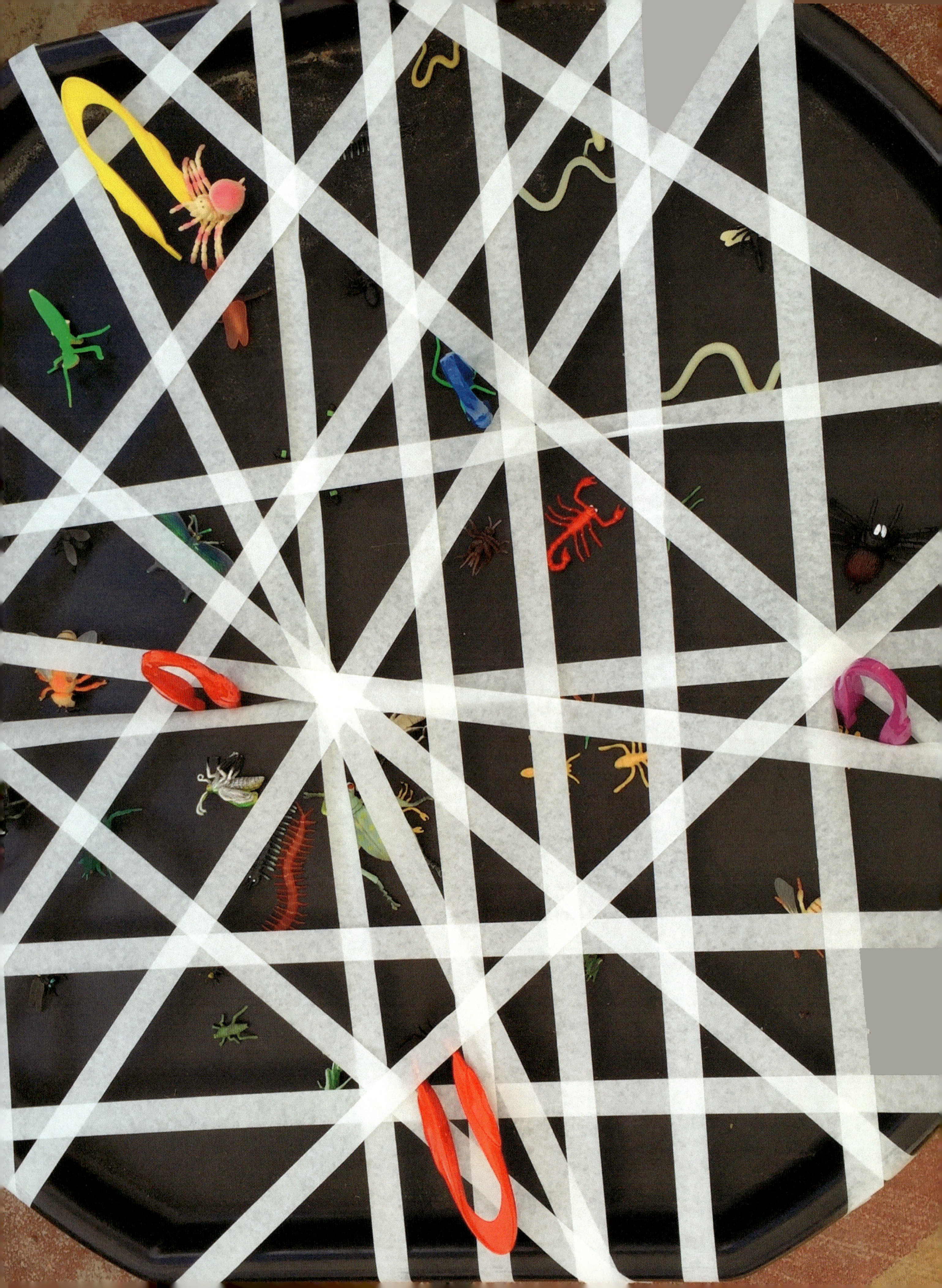

Challenge: **Catch the Minibeast**   Suggested Area of Provision: **Investigation**

Enhance with:	Invite your children to:	Other possible enhancements:
- A tuff spot or plastic tray with masking tape attached from one side to the other to look like a web - Magnifying glasses - Books about minibeasts - Containers for sorting - Plastic minibeasts - Tweezers, tongs, pegs	Use the tools provided to remove the minibeasts from the tuff spot or tray, examine them carefully and then sort them into different containers using their own sorting criteria.	- Instead of tuff spot or plastic tray use a washing basket or plastic tidy basket and weave with string or ribbon across the top to make the web.

Select From the Following Suggested Focused Learning Possibilities

Personal, Social & Emotional Development Making Relationships	Physical Development Moving and Handling	Mathematics Shape, Space & Measure
Use this challenge to: Provide opportunities for your children to practise taking turns and playing co-operatively.	**Use this challenge to…** Provide opportunities for your children to develop their fine motor skills.	**Use this challenge to:** Provide opportunities for your children to use and apply mathematical language.
I am learning to… - join in with others during my play (30-50) - play in a group (30-50) - start a conversation and listen to what others say (40 - 60)	**I am learning to…** - control small equipment (22-36) - use one handed tools (30-50) - control and manipulate different tools safely (40 - 60)	**I am learning to…** - use prepositional words (30-50) - use prepositions to describe where something is (40-60) - use the correct vocabulary to talk about position (ELG)
	Challenge your children to: Use more challenging tools to catch their minibeasts e.g. chopsticks etc.	**Challenge your children to:** - Sort the minibeasts they find into groups using their own criteria. - Catch as many minibeasts as they can in a specified time.

Characteristics of Effective Learning:

Engagement: I am learning to tackle things that may be difficult
Motivation: I am learning to concentrate
Thinking: I am learning to think of my own ideas

Mark Making/Writing Opportunities

Invite your children to:
- Find a way to record the minibeasts that they catch

Enhancing Provision Through Minibeasts

Other Books
by Nicky Simmons and Ginny Morris

Available Now....

Planning for Learning in Early Years (published 2016)

New Series - LEARNING IN EARLY YEARS

Available soon....

Enhancing Provision Through Superheroes

Enhancing Provision Through Under the Sea

Enhancing Provision Through Dinosaurs

Enhancing Provision Through Monsters

Enhancing Provision Through Space

Enhancing Provision Through Traditional Tales

Enhancing Provision Through Nursery Rhymes

Enhancing Provision Through Growing

Printed in Great Britain
by Amazon